A China Adoption Story
Mommy, Why Do We Look Different?

by Frances M. Koh
Illustrated by Anne Sibley O'Brien

Azalea Books
EastWest Press

With thanks to: Sherri Linsenbach, Anne Sibley O'Brien, and
Laurie Ramirez for their contributions to the creation of this book.

Library of Congress Catalog Card Number: 00-130562
International Standard Book Number: 0-9606090-9-1 (lib. binding)

Text & cover design by Frances M. Koh
Typeset by TypeCetera, Inc., Minneapolis, MN
Color separations by Spectrum, Inc., Minneapolis, MN

Manufactured in the United States of America
First Edition
08 07 06 05 04 03 02 01 00   RP 10 9 8 7 6 5 4 3 2 1

To all adopted children and their parents.

One day, when Laura Shu-Mei was four years old, she was looking at pictures in her family photo album. Suddenly she realized she looked quite different from her mom and dad. And she wondered why.

"Mommy, why do we look different?" Laura Shu-Mei asked her mom. "You have red hair, and I have black hair. Your eyes are blue, and mine are brown."

Her mom looked surprised. After hesitating a moment her mom said, "You and I don't look alike, because you were born in China. People in China have black hair and brown eyes. Many times I told you that you were adopted from China, because we loved you very much. You already know that, don't you?"

"Uh, huh," Laura said. "Where is China?"

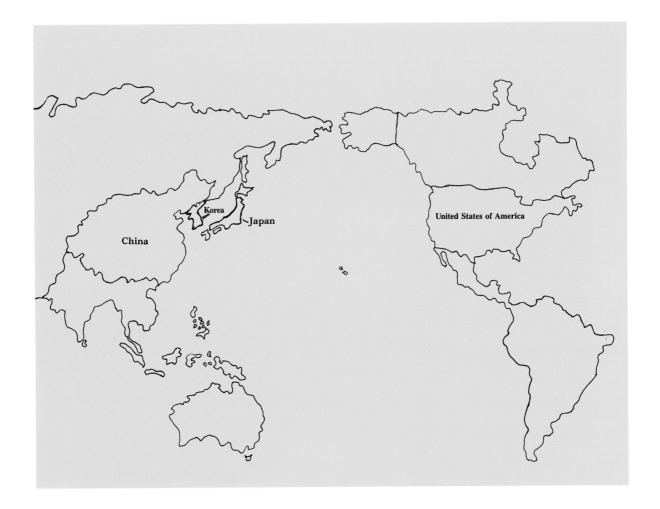

"China is far, far away—halfway around the world. It is the largest country in Asia. It is one of the oldest countries in the world. Lots and lots of people live there. Many millions of people! Their culture is very, very old and amazing. Their Great Wall and Forbidden City are famous and amazing!" her mom said.

"Why didn't I stay in China?" asked Laura.

"Your mom in China was very young when she had you. And, for many reasons, she couldn't take care of you. But she loved you very much and wanted you to have a loving family who would care for you. Your mom knew that the orphanages found families for many children like you. So she placed you at an orphanage, knowing they would care for you and find a family for you too.

"You lived in the orphanage with other children.
There, the nurses cared for you, until they brought us
together. Then your dad and I went to China to bring
you home to live with us."

"Are there other children like me from China?"
asked Laura.

"Yes, many children were born in China like you and now are loved by their families in America," said her mom.

"Why didn't they stay with their mommies in China?" asked Laura.

"Their moms loved their babies very much but couldn't keep them. Each mom had different reasons."

"Why did you want me to come live with you?" asked Laura.

Traditionally, peonies symbolize prosperity in China.

"Your dad and I wanted a little girl to love and care for," her mom said. "We went to a place called an adoption agency. We asked them to help us find a child. We wanted a very special little girl.

"One day the adoption agency worker called. She said they had a very special little girl! They sent us a picture of you and the doctor's report. Just a minute," her mom said. "Hand me the photo album."

Her mom flipped through the pages of the photo album. "Look, here is the picture of you as a baby! Your dad and I thought you were just right for us. And we loved you at once.

"One day the agency called to say that we could go to China and bring you home. Your dad and I went to China by a big airplane. Then we took the train to the town where you lived.

"When we arrived at your orphanage, you were in your room and playing in your crib with a toy. We were so happy to meet you. I lifted you up from your crib and held you in my arms and hugged you. 'Hi, Sweetie,' I said. 'At last we are here to take you home.' Your dad held your tiny hand in his and said, 'Hi! Now you belong in our family!'

"Then we met officials at the provincial office of your hometown. We gave you a new name. We signed papers to have permission to take you home with us. We got your passport and adoption certificate with your new name.

"Your Chinese name was 'Shu Mei' (淑美). That means 'gentle beauty.' We thought it a lovely name and decided to keep it as your middle name. We gave you an American first name—'Laura'—since you will live in America with your family. We think your Chinese and American names together make them sound lovely. Your name is very special—just like you!

The character 淑 (shu) means "gentle"; the character 美 (mei) means either "beautiful" or "beauty", depending on a given context. Since the two characters (淑美) are used here as a female name, they can mean "gentle beauty" or "gentle and beautiful."

"We came home to America by taking a big airplane. During the long ride on the airplane, you and mommy slept together on the passengers' seats.

"At the airport your grandparents, aunts and uncles waited for us. When they met us, I was holding you in my arms. They all surrounded you and said, 'Hi, Sweetie! Welcome home!'

"Laura, I love your brown eyes and black shiny hair, and your lovely smile and your friendly nature. You and I may not look alike, but we are family, bound by love. We belong to each other. We love each other, just as we are. And I love you—just as you are," her mom said. Then she gave Laura a big hug.

Her mom's hug made Laura feel happy and secure. "Mommy," Laura said, "I love you—just as you are."

About the Author

Frances Koh is the author of numerous books for children, including *Adopted from Asia: How It Feels to Grow Up in America, Korean Holidays & Festivals, Korean Games,* and *English-Korean Picture Dictionary.* She is also the author of two books for adults: *Oriental Children in American Homes: How do they adjust?* and *Creative Korean Cooking.* With her first book, *Oriental Children in American Homes,* she received nation-wide recognition. Her other interests are photography and writing short stories. Currently she is at work on several children's story books.

About the Illustrator

Anne Sibley O'Brien is the illustrator of more than twenty books for children, including *Welcoming Babies, Talking Walls, Jamaica and Brianne,* and *Juanah, A Hmong Cinderella.* She also adapted and illustrated a Korean folktale, *The Princess and the Beggar.* In 1997, she and Margy Burns Knight won the National Education Association's Author-Illustrator Human & Civil Rights Award for the body of their work. She was raised in South Korea as the daughter of medical missionaries, and currently lives with her family on Peaks Island in Maine. In 1986 she returned to Korea with her husband and son to bring home her seven-month-old daughter.

A China Adoption Story
Mommy, Why Do We Look Different?
Frances M. Koh
Illustrated by Anne Sibley O'Brien

This book can be ordered from EastWest Press
P.O. Box 14149, Minneapolis, MN 55414
Phone 612/379-2049